I0606155

Transformers

by Julie Murray

Abdo Kids Jumbo is an Imprint of Abdo Kids
abdobooks.com

abdobooks.com

Published by Abdo Kids, a division of ABDO, P.O. Box 398166, Minneapolis, Minnesota 55439.

Printed in the United States of America, North Mankato, Minnesota.

102025

012026

Photo Credits: AdobeStock, Alamy, Everette Collection, Getty Images, Shutterstock, ©mechnine p.7/CC BY 2.0, ©MicroBry p.7/CC BY-NC 2.0, ©mdverde p.13/CC BY-NC-SA 2.0, ©Ben (Falcifer) p.15/CC BY-NC 2.0, ©Gustavo Vargas p.17/CC BY-NC-SA 2.0

Production Contributors: Teddy Borth, Jennie Forsberg, Grace Hansen
Design Contributors: Candice Keimig, Pakou Moua

Library of Congress Control Number: 2025936498

Publisher's Cataloging-in-Publication Data

Names: Murray, Julie, author.

Title: Transformers / by Julie Murray

Description: Minneapolis, Minnesota : Abdo Kids, 2026 | Series: Toy mania! | Includes online resources and index.

Identifiers: ISBN 9798384907619 (lib. bdg.) | ISBN 9798384908319 (ebook) | ISBN 9798384908661 (read-to-me ebook)

Subjects: LCSH: Transformers (Fictitious characters)--Juvenile literature. | Robots--Juvenile literature. | Action figures (Toys)--Juvenile literature. | Hasbro Entertainment (Firm)--Juvenile literature. | Toys--Juvenile literature. | Toys--History--Juvenile literature.

Classification: DDC 688.728--dc23

Table of Contents

Transformers 4

The Making of Generation 1 6

Continued Success 16

More Facts 22

Glossary 23

Index 24

Abdo Kids Code. 24

Transformers

Transformers are alien robots that can **disguise** themselves as different objects. They are 2-in-1 toys that have **transformed** the toy world!

The Making of Generation 1

Many years ago, the Japanese toy company Takara created two toy lines of **transformable** robots. These toys would **inspire** the Transformers toys kids know today.

建設車ロボ

都市の

いる

力な

ロボ

隊で

Micromen

トレインロボ

かねてより開発の続けられていた新6車輌が遂に完成！トレインロボ隊、独自の広範囲にわたる守備力がより充実。建設車ロボ隊と共に6体合体パワーで、敵を迎え撃て!!

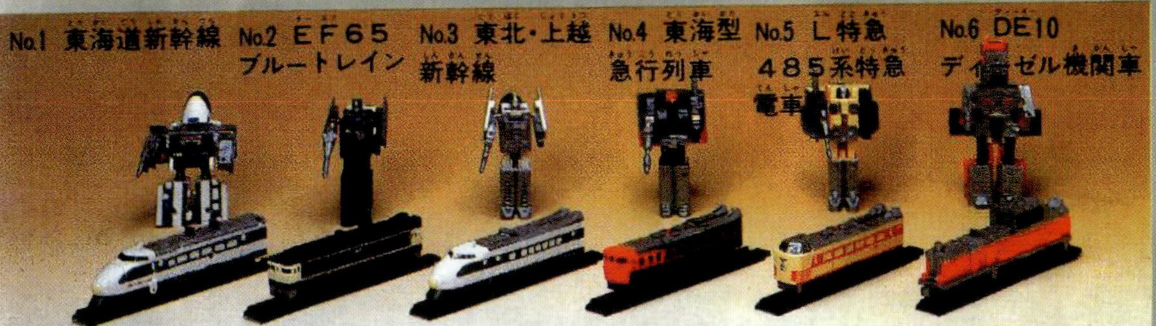

No.1 東海道新幹線

No.2 EF65 ブルートレイン

No.3 東北・上越新幹線

No.4 東海型急行列車

No.5 L特急485系特急電車

No.6 DE10ディーゼル機関車

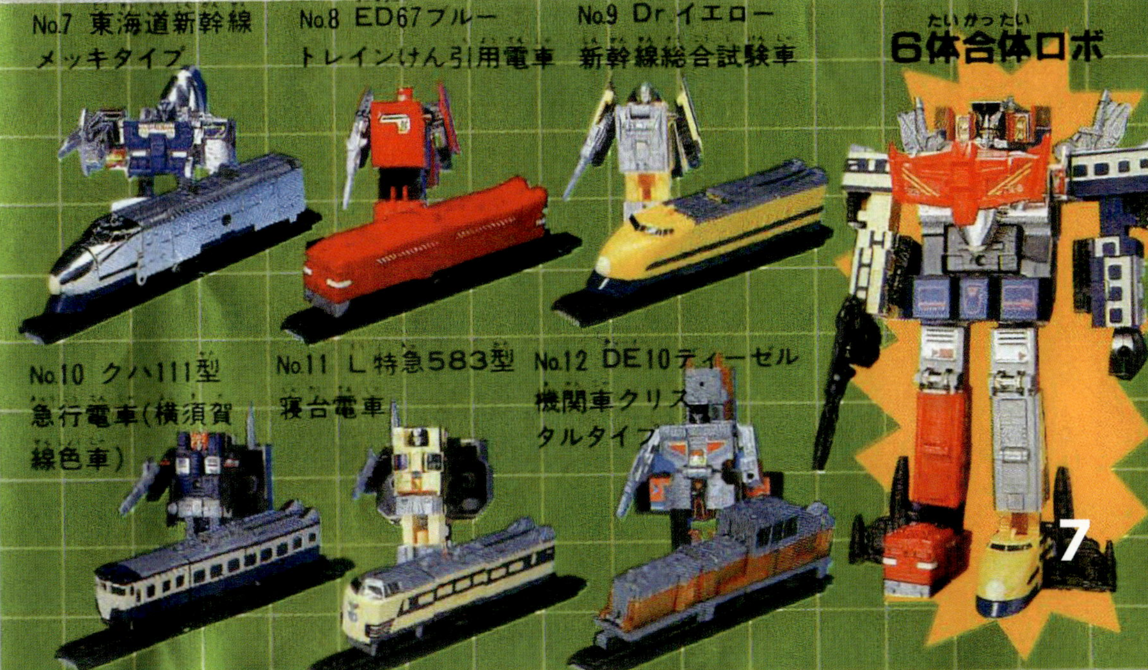

No.7 東海道新幹線メッキタイプ

No.8 ED67ブルートレインけん引用電車

No.9 Dr.イエロー新幹線総合試験車

6体合体ロボ

No.10 クハ111型急行電車(横須賀線色車)

No.11 L特急583型寝台電車

No.12 DE10ディーゼル機関車クリスタルタイプ

Hasbro, an American toy company, bought the rights to the Japanese toys. The first Transformers toys were released in 1984. Hasbro then teamed up with Marvel Comics.

DW
TRANSFORMERS
1 APR
$2.95 US
MARVEL
MORE THAN MEETS THE EYE
THE TRANSFORMERS
75¢ U.K. 40p CAN. 95¢
14 MAR

Marvel **debuted** Transformers comic books and a cartoon series in 1984. These helped introduce the characters and their **backstories** to kids.

The first Transformers toys were called Generation 1. There were 28 figures in all. They were released between 1984 and 1990. They were some of the most popular toys of the 1980s!

Transformers are special because they can change forms. They have movable parts that can slide, twist, and bend. Optimus Prime can go from robot to semitrailer truck!

Continued Success

Over the years, different toy lines have been made. The figures come in many sizes. The 2025 Transformers: Age of the Primes toy line had robots that changed into an airplane, a race car, and a dinosaur!

TRANSFORMERS
AUTOBOT POWERGLIDE
WINDCHARGER
BOMBSHELL
THUNDERCRACKER
STEELJAW
AGES 5+
Mr. Potato Head
PROTECTOBOTS
EMERGENCY RESPONSE
AGES 6+
PROTECTOBOTS
EVAC SQUAD
AGES 6+
PLATINUM EDITION
DINOBOTS UNLEASHED 5-PACK
AGES 8+
GRIMLOCK
Hasbro

Many Transformers movies and TV shows have come out over the years. They have brought fresh characters into the world of Transformers. Because of this, new toys hit the shelves each year.

Transformers continue to be popular today. Their exciting stories and special skills have entertained people for more than 40 years!

More Facts

- *Transformers*: The Ride – 3D first opened at Universal Studios Singapore in 2011. Since then, the ride has also come to the California and Florida locations.

- There have been many Transformers movies. The first **live-action** film, *Transformers*, came out in 2007.

- The Transformers toy line was **inducted** into the National Toy Hall of Fame in 2024.

Glossary

backstory – a story about the things that led up to the main story.

debuted – presented for the first time.

disguise – to hide one's identity.

inducted – brought in as a member.

inspire – to give a new idea for something creative.

live-action – of, relating to, or featuring action involving real people or animals.

transform – to change form, look, or shape.

Index

comic books 10

Generation 1 12

Hasbro 8

Japan 6, 8

Marvel Comics 8, 10

movies 18

Optimus Prime 14

Takara 6

television 10, 18

Transformers: Age of the Primes 16